Soul Imprints

An Overview of Psychobiology and Genetic Resonance

Roberta Maria Atti

for Sydney, Hugo, Elliot, Rexy, Cape and Cod with my
deepest gratitude

Roberta Maria Atti

P.O. Box 1258

Maplewood, NJ 07040

www.creativehealthsolutions.org

Copyright© 2006 by Roberta Maria Atti

ISBN: 978-0-6151-5146-5

TABLE OF CONTENTS

Introduction

Dedicated to all those who ask me... "but what is it exactly that you do?"

My work, for the past several years, has been centered around one goal: helping people familiarize with the most effective therapeutic modalities available, in order to achieve physical, emotional, mental and spiritual well being. Inspired by the newest perspectives in psychobiology, intergenerational genetic resonance and molecular medicine, my outlook is based on the lifelong research of several medical scholars and pioneers.

Health care costs have reached an all time high, while statistics show an increase in the incidence of all major killer diseases. We keep suffering needlessly, in spite of the trillions of dollars spent in treatment research. What you are about to read, a description of psychobiological patterns and related information, is impeccably congruent with the latest discoveries in physics, sociology, evolution, genealogy, and psychoneuroimmunology.

The therapeutic interventions stemming from this research are designed to facilitate the surfacing of blind and compelling ancestral dynamics, usually hidden in a person's unconscious and out of reach of the reasoning mind. These broken pieces of our unknown self, inherited and never acknowledged, have the power to affect us in ways that can be baffling at best, tragic at worst, until they are addressed, released and integrated with the rest of who we are.

This piece of common sense used to be well known and taken into account by health practitioners of traditional and tribal medicine, and this is true for every culture, continent and community, everywhere in the world, up until very recently. Unfortunately for us, our high-tech medical approach has altogether discarded, if not criminalized, the implementation of powerful ritualistic therapeutic modalities designed to untangle these inherited soul knots. And so we treat people by giving them colorful pills with names like Allegra®, all the while ignoring that most illnesses seem to begin with a broken heart.

Life flows forth as an evolving organism that stretches in time like a tree stretches in space. Based on that metaphor, we are not a separate unit of life, as we have been taught in this Cartesian educational system of ours, but rather we can be compared to a branch on our family's tree. This unbreakable and invisible bond we have been ignoring acts like a conduit of information on all levels: genetic, physical, emotional, mental, sexual and everything else.

It seems that this information resonates, from within our DNA, with the psychogenetic structure we share with our current family members, as well as members in the past and future. We are therefore a recipient for, and container of, our family's recorded destiny and history, including whatever suffering has not yet been healed in the morphogenetic field affecting, informing and belonging to, each and everyone of its members.

Based on this outlook, once we are willing to acknowledge these inherited "entanglements", once we stop ignoring them, we may have already diminished their pathological potential. And if, motivated by selfhealing intentions, we honor those family members (and related aspects of ourselves) that have been estranged, we may then recover an inner fluidity and vitality impossible to achieve otherwise.

Once the burden of plurigenerational suffering is taken off our backs, we are finally able to stand tall, maybe for the first time in our lives, and see the true horizon of who we are, with all if its potential for joy and freedom, as well as health and harmony.

In this way, the most important gift we have ever received, the vital energy given to us by our predecessors, can finally be released from the past, rejoin and enliven our bodies and minds in the present and be available, in its entirety, for future generations.

Are our children worthy of this effort on our part? The answer, I believe, speaks loudly within our hearts.

"Birth", by Roberta Maria Atti
Artist and Photographer

Chapter 1

Self-Consciousness

Consciousness, in reference to the human mind, describes the reflective perceptual dynamic emergent at the center of the mental structure we call "self". At times we experience it sequentially, not unlike a series of chronological movie frames. Most of the times simultaneously, as an evolving awareness of the people, objects and events we encounter in our life.

What makes it so interesting is that every center of consciousness is unequivocally unique and this is true not just at the human level. No two moments, people, places, events, organisms, objects, grains of sand, solar systems or galaxies.... could ever be identical, throughout our infinite universe. From this observation we can endlessly speculate, resolving to believe, for instance, that creation is equally conscious of itself, everywhere and at every moment. But, at least for now, these are suppositions and cannot be considered facts.

The human "self", reflectively aware of its uniqueness, is born from and grows surrounded by other selves, interdependent on one another and similarly conscious and unique. For humans, the self becomes the referential psychosomatic center of being, barring events that affect memory and/or perception. The child learns to locate his or her own particular unit of consciousness by identification with a physical image, as well as with the ever growing storehouse of memories, thoughts and ideas held within his or her mind.

The totality of these factors, coherently organized, becomes a mental representation of who we are. This mental state can be likened to an active morphogenetic field, in the sense that, believing in the image we paint of ourselves as if it were objectively true, our mind shapes our physical self in accordance with whom it believes it to be. This mental image, reflected outwardly, becomes a visible expression of the self we create day after day, inclusive of conscious and unconscious aspects.

In infancy we have almost no "self" consciousness, and that is when humans look alike more than at any other time in life. Individual animals, even among the higher primates, look more like one another, since the adult's mental content does not separate nor differentiate much from the group's. This is because animals, still functioning from within a group soul, share a common morphogenetic field as a matrix for psychosomatic development and self-expression. It's different for humans.

As we grow and discover who we are, we individualize and differentiate from everyone else, because we are the product of our own unique soul blueprint. The longer we live, the more our facial expression, reflective of how we feel about life, becomes etched onto our facial structure. We look the way our mind believes we feel, based on our life experiences and what we think they mean.

In infancy mental activity is automatic and mostly unconscious. The human mind learns to define and refine the emerging self, similar to a sculptor working on a chunk of marble, by shaping and chipping away what is not self while allowing the inner soul's qualities to be revealed outwardly, from within the flesh.

The mental self, expressed by the biochemistry of the nervous and immune systems for instance, reacts to chemical signals at the cellular level and responds by selecting what must be kept and what must be eliminated at the molecular level. My belief is that it is capable of doing this with such amazing accuracy and determination because it is instructed by an invisible blueprint.

This blueprint defines the potential of who the self is meant to become, and we used to think this information, spelled out from birth, was held more or less safely within the genes. Recent theories are beginning to question our assumptions in this regard, however, and some scientists place the self's operational headquarters altogether outside the body.

Regardless of where it is, the infant's mind, not yet able to perform as a unit of consciousness, is the instrument the baby uses to accomplish the task of individuation. He or she cannot perceptually separate from the surroundings and therefore cannot mentally or physically differentiate from everything else: in simpler terms, the infant is conscious, but not yet self-conscious.

At this stage, however, the self operates mostly within the autonomic nervous system. It takes care of automatic functions, like digestion and temperature regulation and fosters individuation, whereby, slowly, the child learns to distinguish self from others. Unconscious and subconscious mental activity happens quietly within cellular life, while the baby learns where self begins and where it ends, and not always without a power struggle.

The separated self begins to stir in the mind of the young human, physically through the development of the immune system. This is the system in charge of establishing clearer and firmer individual markers. Its task is to separate the baby from maternal life first and from the rest of life subsequently.

Life begins without self-consciousness in the young mind. The mind awakens to its own boundaries and the ego learns to define itself while the digestive system and metabolic functions transmute food into energy, the muscular/skeletal system stretches and grows, increasing body mass, and the immune/nervous system integrates memory bits, labeling them with "self" markers, claiming ownership, investing its time and energy in the development of a "self" conscious being by selecting what to re-member and what to forget of its daily life.

While at first everything seems to blend into one undiffer-entiated perceptual viewpoint, growth and development can happen only by outcasting the world in favor of the personal "self". The process is akin to an eviction: aware-ness of the world as self shrinks while self-awareness grows. As babies, the world contains us. We are "it", not a piece of it. We don't know we have a name, an address, a unique body that will never merge with anything while liv-ing. We see everything as a whole, of which we are an as-pect, not a part.

But eventually we grow and develop a different percep-tion: as adults we contain the world, in the form of an idea, and we relate to it as if it were external to us. The world becomes smaller, in importance, as our self grows bigger, even though realize how tiny we are, in terms of our size. It is true that the more we grow the further we are able to reach with our explorations. But our inner self grows more important and so it is for its needs.

Babies' mental and physical needs are simple and basic. Adults needs can get quite complex: a personal territory, recognition, comfort, power, companionship, control, affection, success, proficiency, reassurance, validation, money, status, security, not to mention education, food, shelter, love and safety.

Self-consciousness develops as a result of incessant testing and adjusting of our unique perspective as we grow, negotiating and eventually mastering our interactions with the rest of the world. Through interacting with an outside reality, or rather our internalized picture of it, we create a "self" that fits in with what we believe we are surrounded by.

To the extent that we separate from what is not us, we create an identity that is at the center of the universe, quite literally. While living, we make choices that seem to shape our destiny and thus we discover who we are in relation to life. Simple enough, at least until we are confronted with parts of us that clash with the world, those aspects of our "self" that lurk in the shadows, like strange creatures at the bottom of our ocean-like mind.

What happens when we find a "self" we are not familiar and/or comfortable with? That is where, for many people, trouble begins. Because that is when we are compelled to project this shadow onto our neighbors, thereby outcasting our unwanted self.

Not too long ago religion may have been the source of guidance most people sought when facing the self that betrays, abandons, shames, ridicules, attacks, resents, criticizes, blames, condemns, judges, obsesses, defies and destroys the goodness in us and in those we love. We have been told, by the wise among us, that those whom we call our enemies, are but a reflection of our disowned self.

And yet, when confronted with hurtful behavior on the part of others, we find it almost impossible to look at the mirror we are facing. This bigger, more accurate reality, emerging from scientific observation, irrational and paradoxical in the extreme, whereby what we encounter is inevitably but an aspect of ourselves, is difficult to understand, let alone accept.

Psychotherapy may be the choice these days. A more humanistic path perhaps, given religions' almost unforgivable failures and mistakes. Yet, the unredeemable self still haunts us, under the guise of a wicked other, unscathed and unfettered by our attempts to dispose of it through crusades of morality, religious fervor and just wars.

The monster is still at large, getting bigger and meaner. I do not wish to entertain images of doom. I cannot deny, however, that hostility has reached epidemic proportions and no one seems to know quite what to do about the violence that has become like a modern plague, if not respond to it with more violence and bigger weapons.

I suggest that the problem may be different from what we believe it to be. Since violence doesn't seem to end using violence as a cure for it, I wonder how we would respond to it if we came to accept that our unique self, whose boundaries and possessions we fight over, sometimes to the death, was never meant to function as a separate unit.

Modern physics shows interconnectedness, not just among fellow humans, but with other forms of life, plants and animals, and even with the mineral world or with the stars up above, things we have not considered conscious until now, and yet, are beginning to emerge in our awareness as kin, rather than inert matter.

Humans have been taught to think and behave as separate units of consciousness, whereas human lives are tightly interwoven and human choices affects not just other humans but everything else on the planet. The illusion that we are separate is all pervasive, seems impossible to eradicate and continues to cause much avoidable suffering. But something within us is changing, even as we struggle to define what that is.

Given that we are all made of the same stuff, humans, plants and stars alike, it doesn't take much effort to accept the possibility that we may be endless variations of one thing. The most apparently insignificant choice towards kindness, or carelessness, as intangible and invisible as one thought, has an effect on the whole, we now know from scientific observation. The effect may be undetectable on a small scale, but the cumulative results of our communal choices and tendencies are readily measurable by modern technological sensitivity.

Perhaps a good metaphor for the concept of "self" is that of a thread in a cotton cloth: unique, similarly constructed, made from the same raw material, interwoven with, and yet separate from, all other threads.

Imagine holding one single cotton thread in your right hand, a cotton cloth in your left hand, and notice how one thread on its own feels very different from a thread woven into the cloth. Both threads have identical structure and characteristics. However, the significance of one thread is not fully grasped until the thread is used to support a structure, such as a cloth, comprised of many units like itself. Is the thread sacrificed or actualized when woven into the cloth? It depends on the perspective.

Sensitive recording equipment has been set up all over the world to measure the effect of human consciousness in relation to world events. So far we have not come to a definite conclusion, but there seems to be a clear correlation between collective human thought and what goes on on the planet. It will not be much longer, I believe, before we are able to confirm it beyond doubt.

Intuition has been whispering in our ears what the great minds have taught and modern physics demonstrates: that the undesirable reality we sometimes find ourselves trapped in could be the result of cumulative self-centered acts based on fear and greed caused, in part, by our choice of consciousness. This is the "self-consciousness" choice whereby we exist in competition, rather than cooperation, with other life forms and with one another.

The difference in scale is so great that we have been unable to make the connection until now. It seems impossible, in the drop of resentment or prejudice I allow myself to feel towards my neighbor, that I may be contributing to create a bloody war on the other side of the globe. And yet, that is precisely the missing piece, or perhaps the missing peace, of our human puzzle.

Given the global challenges we are faced with at this time, it seems desirable to develop a kind of "self consciousness" that includes possibilities beyond our usual perception. And that is, to a great extent, the purpose of my explorations.

Given the current outlook for the future, it is practically impossible to find writings that are both realistic and optimistic. Maybe I am too ambitious, but I am attempting to do just that. I have great appreciation for humanity and faith in its ability to learn from mistakes.

Let's imagine, for argument's sake, that, rather than a single, separate being, I am one cell functioning within a community of cells (a multicellular organism), all with similar qualities, needs and goals. This exercise may seem futile at first, but soon enough it becomes apparent that, if we functioned from that perspective, our lives would become easier and safer, not to mention more abundant: it doesn't take a genius to see how, by tending to the needs of the whole, our own needs are automatically taken care of, and without much effort.

If we continue to explore what "self" is, perhaps, we might be able to expand our understanding of it and eventually arrive at a mode of selfconsciousness that doesn't lead to separateness and selfdestructiveness. My hope is that, through creativity and with faith in ourselves, we may be able to bring about a wonderful future for our children.

MENTAL HEALTH

The mind, body, spirit and emotions are inseparable. Like players in a team, they can be isolated and observed separately, but we cannot expect to fully understand their role unless we take into account the whole team. Psychotherapy cannot be purely mental or emotional, detached from body and spirit: integration is necessary.

In our search for a therapeutic model that works in today's world, we must start by critiquing the prevailing styles of psychotherapy, not so much to devalue, but rather in an attempt to improve their effectiveness.

As we explore the clinical approach to mental illness in its practical applications, the model we are most likely to encounter seems to be but an offshoot of current medical paradigms: it is as if our soul struggles were just one more form of pathology, to be eradicated by any means necessary, for the soul's own benefit and for the good of humanity.

Unfortunately, or perhaps fortunately for us, the human soul refuses to be conscripted within such limits. This is clearly demonstrated by our ineffectiveness at establishing adequate levels of social sanity.

Given the vast improvement we have witnessed, this may sound like an unfair assessment: however, serious mental pathology is not relegated to mental hospitals and may be at play in many of the dynamics we accept as the unnecessary unpleasantness we don't normally think of as insane. How mentally sound is it to turn mental hospitals into homeless shelters, for one thing? And so on and so forth.

Mental illness manifests as a destructive force in individuals and communities, tearing into the matrix of life itself. It suffocates hope, joy, compassion and creativity. Mental illness confuses us with half truths and false enlightenment. All we seem to be able to do, more often than not, is prescribe mind altering drugs, clinging to the belief that numbness may be our only salvation.

But addressing global sanity is too large an endeavor at this point. Let's start by focusing on the individual, the person who suffers with emotional and mental pain, the soul who is looking for an answer to life's irreducible dilemma. The one who seems to be lost in paradox and confusion, struggling to find balance on the tight rope of existence, often afraid to take a step forward or back.

Chapter 2

DNA Resonance and Behavioral Patterns

I first heard about genetic resonance patterns from my sister. She would call me from Italy to tell me about some new and rather unusual workshops she had attended, where she had been given an opportunity to look at herself from a completely different perspective.

Having devoted my life to the healing arts and being endlessly fascinated with anything people use to heal themselves, I would listen to her enthusiastic descriptions and soon became intrigued with the possibilities, wondering how I could find a way to experience the same kind of process myself. Shortly thereafter I was invited to attend a Family Constellations workshop with Bert Hellinger and had a chance to have my wishes granted.

As soon as the first family constellation was staged in front of my eyes I realized I was witnessing something exceptional, and now it became not only interesting but a powerful new experience that commanded my full attention. What could have touched me so deeply, I wondered, as I watched that first piece of intergenerational drama unfold a few feet away from me. What was happening to those strangers, on that dimly lit auditorium stage, that I should feel so invested in the outcome of it, as if it had been my own family whose life wounds were being touched?

The process addressed the ongoing suffering of a woman whose relatives had been killed in concentration camps. The small group on stage consisted of a few representatives for her family members and the same number of representatives for their murderers. Everyone seemed to know exactly what the person they were representing would have felt in that situation and each representative expressed those feelings with an accuracy and spontaneity worthy of a professional actor.

The fairly young woman for whom this work was being done had been suffering from various symptoms, physical and emotional, that would not improve with anything she had done up to this point. Her question to Bert Hellinger addressed the possibility that she was still carrying grief and rage in relation to these ancestors of hers, all of whom she had never met.

At first, when the process began, everyone on stage obediently followed the succinct instructions of this rather unceremonious 80 year old man, as if they had been rehearsing their part in a play he was directing. However, once everyone had taken his or her place on stage, Bert stopped giving directions, sat down, and simply started to observe the representatives, all of whom remained immobile, simply looking at one another, for quite a long time.

Or so it seemed to the inexperienced eye. Actually, even while everything seems to be at a standstill in a constellation, barely perceptible movements begin to stir, what Hellinger calls "movements of the soul". A hand might contract into a fist. Shoulders might drop slightly. Knees might bend or straighten. Eyes might fill with tears. All of it means that something is coming to the surface, in order to be released and hopefully brought to a permanent resolution.

After a rather long prelude of pregnant silence, interactions among members of the group on stage became very dynamic and one could feel an increasingly intense emotional current overtaking the entire auditorium, including the onlooking audience. Everyone was deeply involved. Everyone as quietly focused as I was.

I felt certain, much to my surprise, that we all seemed to be hoping for a compassionate outcome, whereby everyone involved, no matter what they had done, could find peace, along with everyone else. We seemed to hope for a greater justice than the eye for an eye kind of justice and I remember noticing how unusual that was, given the self-righteous approach of traditional group psychotherapy, whereby one is encouraged, in the name of restoring adequate self-esteem, to find and publicly condemn a certain "culprit".

And herein, in my view, lies one of the most powerfully therapeutic aspects of this process: it doesn't look for ancestors to punish, people to blame, parents to crucify, caretakers who neglected us, those who abandoned us when we needed them the most, so that we can feel justified in our hatred and bitterness towards them.

Rather, it fosters a kind of leveling of the human spirit, whereby we are encouraged to look at, and honor, everyone's humanity, even in the case of those who behaved cruelly towards us. Not out of a sentimental need to forgive and forget where responsibility belongs. On the contrary, to acknowledge whose actions, and relative consequences, belong to whom, return whatever negative feelings we may still be holding in relation to those actions and people and set ourselves free from carrying the emotional burden entangled with other people's mistakes.

Being someone who has seen and experienced so many different therapeutic modalities I am no longer naïve, nor am I easily sold on something, simply because someone says, "it's great," not even when it's my own sister saying it. I must see and decide for myself, if I am to be convinced. Well, I was convinced. Right from that initial experience with this process I sensed a potential in it that I had not perceived elsewhere and I decided to understand what it was about.

"Cosmic Love", by Roberta Maria Atti
Artist and Photographer

Chapter 3

Mythical Genes and Genetic Myths

The human mind lives within a myth, creating and recreating it while participating in the drama of daily events. We could say we are given a script at the moment we are conceived and act it out as we evolve and live.

We do have some choice over how we play our role. Not much, but some. The myth serves as an outline, but we are allowed, within certain limits, to improvise. The basic plot, what we need to know in order to survive on earth, is specified in our genetic manual, our DNA. We live/play/act the myth as we live and sometimes we get carried away with improvisation, fall off the stage and disappear amidst the choreography.

Everything we experience while acting out our myth, physically or emotionally, is explained and categorized according to pre-established codes we carry within our cells, recorded onto our life's textbook, passed on to us by our ancestors, through millions of years of trial and error, success and failure, life and death on earth.

This very small package of essential information, this molecular "Life Instruction Manual", or LIM, is given to us by our parents at the moment of our conception. They, in turn, got their LIM from their parents, and so on and so forth. Each generation adds a few words to it, perhaps only a few letters, and so it is that life evolves and keeps a record of how it manages to negotiate the odds, even in the most unfavorable circumstances.

One word after another, a million years after another, a billion people after another, and we end up with a meticulously selected collection of genetic instructions. Our DNA brings forward the knowledge of essential, collective and individual choices that have shaped the human experience, thereby becoming memories. When the memories are contained in our DNA they are called genetic, because they are given to us through genes, units of information encoded in light messages, contained within our parents' cells and united at the moment we are conceived.

The totality of the human experience, contained in the parents' DNA, joins to create a reconfiguration of itself in the baby's DNA. During nine months of gestation, while the new life develops safely within mother's inner ocean, the baby's organism is given a review of life's evolution on earth, all the way from single cell to most evolved organism.

At birth the little person has lived through all of the major evolutionary landmarks: from unicellular to multicellular, to fish, amphibian, bird, mammal and finally human, which is so close to a chimpanzee that one wonders how can so little structural difference create such a huge gap in development. What we see, however, is the result of a tiny difference over a long period of time, and this is an important thing to notice. At the beginning of a divergence the space between two lines could be insignificant but the further along we go, the wider it becomes.

Our "self", the unit of consciousness in charge of our being, develops in part through deciphering the genetic instructions received at conception. As we grow and develop, we learn what it means to be human, in general, and, specifically, what it means to be one particular human being.

This happens thanks to gene activation, modulation and expression. Some genes remain dormant for a life time, while some are activated from day one. What we think, feel, see, imagine, prefer to drink, eat, touch and otherwise perceive, communicate and express determines, to a great extent, what we encounter in life and how we define ourselves through it.

Through current research we are now discovering that we have a lot more control over what happens to us than previously believed, precisely because we can choose which aspects of our genetic reservoir we want to bring to light through behavior and lifestyle choices, and which we prefer to keep dormant. Recent discoveries show that genetic predisposition to disease do not justify living in fear and the gloomy predictions of a medical industry that benefits from us being sick do not have to be accepted with blind faith.

A predisposition is comparable to a light switch that we can turn on or off. Certainly our daily dietary choices have something to do with how we express our genetic inheritance. What we drink, inhale and absorb, as well as who we associate with does too. How about what we think? Could that have anything to do with what happens to us?

As it turns out it is true that our thinking exerts a powerful effect on our genetic expression and so what we think, feel, say, create, despise, believe in, disown, acquire, sacrifice, love, hate, desire, blame, control or judge....all of the thoughts and feelings we entertain have an effect on our chemistry and therefore on our genetic expression.

Modern cosmology supports the myth of a humanity in exile from Heaven and most religions confirm it: human beings, body, mind and soul, having lost the right to dwell in the original Garden, are like cosmic refugees.

Trapped in a cage of decaying flesh, the human soul must find its way home, back to bliss and immortality, through the perils and agonies of life on earth. And this is so in spite of cosmogony, which, disguised as scientific discourse, assigns to the human the most evolved form of consciousness in the universe.

In spite of our sophisticated consciousness life on earth is not easy, our DNA warns us. Within its spiraled twirls, we find instructions on how to accomplish daily tasks, as well as special programs that disable and override standard procedures. Some information is there to be accessed only in an emergency, and only when all else fails.

Life programmed the programmer, our mythical DNA, to ignore its own dictates when faced with unforeseen difficulties, something not even nature could have taken into account. In a crisis, there is a point beyond which genetic instructions are useless, except for the fact that they can be disregarded, thereby opening our creative door.

We may have run out of solutions, but creativity never stops. Creativity allows us to write a new human myth, all the way down to our genes, and this can reframe our purpose on earth. The new myth we come up with might save our future and, who knows, perhaps, even our souls.

Our genes are programmed to maintain our bodies in a harmonious exchange of energy with our environment . But if that changes in ways that are not part of the given possibilities, our bodies can no longer simply follow a genetic script. In order to survive we must rewrite our genetic instructions, thereby adapting and evolving.

My personal myth unfolds in front of me like a carpet rolled out under the feet of a special guest. As soon as I step on it, I bring my myth to life. I also irrevocably endorse it to my past. I cannot go back and retrieve it, neither from the present, where I am, nor from the future, where I will be. And here things can get confusing.

If I don't like the consequences of the choices I have made in the past, or if I believe I have been irreparably wounded by others, I cannot feel good about who I am in the present. It seems that the past holds a part of me hostage and won't let it go free. Perhaps this is what Freud called neurosis.

If I cannot separate myself from what has happened to me, if I learn to define my "self" based on what was done to me, or what was taken away, I may lose a very important connection with a deeper truth and end up believing I "am" the loss I measure myself by.

My spouse, parents, children, looks, achievements, illnesses, friends, relationships, education, home, car, job, lifestyle, whatever is visible of me becomes my identity, my way of perceiving myself from within and of describing myself to the outside world.

If I don't know who I am, aside from the relative positives and negatives my image conveys, looking for a deeper sense of self seems useless or even dangerous. A mind that has been built on this kind of reflective structure, based on societal definition, approval or disapproval tends to collapse and get lost in an ocean of self-doubt and fear when things no longer match expectations.

I may lose consciousness of the rest of me, to the point where I am no longer aware of anything but my image. I may feel victimized by my own misguided "self", by other "selves", or it may be tempting to adopt a view whereby my fate was written in the stars from the day I was born.

This perspective saves me from guilt and regrets, but does not help much with bitterness over the inevitable disappointments life presents me with. It also removes creativity from the equation, because if I am willing to blame something other than me for my misfortune, on any level, I must also relinquish the possibility that I may be able to create what I want.

To the degree that I choose not to take responsibility for my suffering I also choose to surrender my power to change things, for better or for worse. Image based self-consciousness is so pervasive that, if I don't look for an alternative, it is almost impossible to envision who I am beyond a quantitative assessment of my good or bad fortune.

Self-consciousness. What is it? What defines me, in my own mind, if not what is visible of me? Is there an invisible essence, a Wizard behind the tent? A "self" that is conscious of existing independently from its container?

If I stand in front of a mirror and say "this is me", is my image telling the truth? Am I? Or is my mind like a kitten, playing with its reflection in a mirror? Similarly to the kitten, sometimes I prefer to keep playing with my image and pretend not to notice how confused and baffled I feel when I find there is no one behind the mirror. What is it I am looking at then? Perhaps the same mind that gives itself a name believes to be what it names.

There is a connection, at least for humans and a few higher primates, between "self" image and the "self" consciousness that perceives the image, but to superimpose the two leads to confusion. Especially when I realize that there is no one behind the mirror, except me, looking for myself in my image.

This "self" I am attempting to define is therefore an elusive concept, a shape shifting aspect of mental representation, an image based on my subjective feelings, a continuously emerging newborn in need of care and mirroring, if it is to survive and maintain its integrity. Perhaps the self is simply the sum of all memories, of what it took for life to be alive here and now, within me.

"Tiger", by Roberta Maria Atti
Artist and Photographer

CHAPTER 4

A Bit of History and Description of Family Constellations and the Intergenerational Resonance Process

Intergenerational resonance has been a fascinating process to explore, I must say, especially once I discovered that its originator, Bert Hellinger, a theologian and pedagogue, has lived for many years with the Zulu Tribe of South Africa, starting out as a missionary and then becoming a member of that community, before studying Western psychology in the US and Europe. In my view, this work results from a combination of tribal medicine wisdom with standard modern psychological form. Hellinger's multifaceted and multilayered background, in my view, is what makes this method so unique.

According to Bert Hellinger, illnesses usually represent a family member. Either a direct relative or someone who got involved with the family (by marriage for instance, but not only) and acquired the same status as a blood relative. An illness can also represent an unfinished emotional sequence, such as an early life abandonment for instance, or a betrayal of a family member by another member.

If a difficult destiny befalls a person, the theory goes, and this is not dealt with appropriately by the rest of the family, (i.e. an ant who might be slightly senile and is committed to an institution prematurely because no one wants to be encumbered by her presence), the family's collective conscience could attempt to address and rectify the injustice by causing another member to suffer, maybe half a century later. While this way of reestablishing equilibrium may seem unfair from a human perspective, we must not forget that the family's soul operates at a level which is above human, or supra-human.

In that realm different rules apply. If, in order for an entire family to regain equilibrium one particular event must be resolved, the soul of the family continues to manifest imbalances in some of its members until the problem is found, acknowledged and brought to a peaceful resolution for everyone involved. And this is true even if the people with whom the problem originates have long ago departed and have never even met those who might be resonating with that suffering today. This is because, according to the proponents of psychobiology, we carry a base memory of everything that has happened in our family within our cellular structure and cannot avoid being affected by this inheritance, for better or worse.

It is difficult for us modern thinkers to accept this kind of explanation, and I have to admit it was not easy for me. But I could not deny what I saw and felt and experienced, all of which confirmed that, as individuals, we do not function in a vacuum. We are rather like branches on a tree and therefore must tend to the health of the whole tree, if we are to thrive.

While this approach is similar to the well known Family Systems Theory, in my opinion it goes much further: in an intergenerational system, we are not only affected horizontally in the timeline, by our immediate family. It could be that the life of one member who lived a hundred years ago, contains the key to our health and well being, affecting us in a vertical timeline direction, because of DNA resonance at the cellular level.

Let's hypothesize that one of our predecessors was abandoned as a baby, before we were born, and never heard from again. That baby is not going to disappear simply because no one wanted him or her at the time. His or her presence persists and it continues to demand proper recognition, if not as a memory, maybe as a gnawing feeling of anxiety, a recurring nightmare, an obsessive thought, an illness, an unusual family bond, a mood that won't let up or a non-specified ghostlike malaise in some other individual belonging to that genealogical tree, until that baby is given a rightful place in the heart of the family, with the same dignity and love as everyone else.

How can we do that if we don't know it happened? How can we give a place in our hearts to a baby we don't even know existed? This is the question people will ask, usually, at this point.

It is a legitimate question and there is no easy way to answer it. We might never find out the specifics, but there is a way whereby we can open our heart to those who have been forgotten, thereby inviting them to come back into the safety and warmth of our family's bosom. While it is impossible to describe the positive shift that takes place when some forgotten member is reunited with us in this way, one only needs to experience it once, or observe someone else go through the experience, to realize that not everything powerful can be verbalized or explained, nor is it always necessary to intellectually understand what happens in order to benefit from an experiential therapeutic process.

This kind of family work goes beyond observing that a child has become the angry scapegoat in a dysfunctional family with an alcoholic parent, for instance. It goes much deeper and much wider than just dealing with the immediacy of the visible pathological dynamics.

Again, I'd like to use my favorite metaphor, in order to explain what occurs. In the same way as a leaf represents the newest life on a tree, and can only live if attached to the tree (the family/organism of origin), a human does not exist in isolation. Since the leaf is attached to a branch, which is an extension of the trunk and root system, if the leaf dries up, for instance, we will not be able, in most cases, to understand what went wrong by looking only at the branch.

Even someone who is not a botanist, would know that we need to inspect the whole tree, in order to find out why a leaf dries up. In fact, we might have to look all the way down into the root system, in order to heal whatever is affecting the leaves. This metaphor, in my view, explains exactly how intergenerational DNA resonance works.

"Heart", by Roberta Maria Atti
Artist and Photographer

Chapter 5

Psychobiology and the physiology of separation

The current disease model says that disease happens randomly, or because of inevitable genetic flaws we have inherited.

The psychobiological model says that disease is a special kind of biological program, implemented by the brain in response to an unforeseen event, something that has happened to us for which we were not prepared.

Not everyone who suffers a trauma develops an illness from it, or the same illness as others who have experienced the same trauma: one person may get sick with one kind of symptom, another person with another kind of symptom and yet another may not get sick at all.

This is because, on the cellular level, we carry different memories, based on our families' histories and unresolved conflicts - we therefore react to life in part from our own memory, what we have learned, but also from what is given to us by our families.

I am not talking about genetic propensities towards certain illnesses - I am referring to a much deeper concept of inherited memory, one that is not yet fully recognized by our medical system - I am referring to the memories that are transferred from one generation to the next via unconscious messages stored in the cellular structure, possibly quantifiable as a molecular frequency.

Depending on what has or has not been resolved in our family, we are going to see reality from a certain perspective: events will be interpreted through the filter of our family's history, successes, failures, losses and struggles, always based on survival strategies that have or have not been effective

What memory is activated in response to trauma? How do we find the original conflict, the moment in which the disease process has begun? Where is the triggering event, the original feeling of something irreparable happening to us, something we couldn't have foreseen and were unprepared for? What was the content of that psychic moment in our mind? What was the feeling in our body? How have we been carrying this emotional burden? What memory is awakened by this event? What kind of belief about ourselves or the world?

Until this is confronted and consciously challenged, it will keep coming up. In fact, we continue to create the same situations, the same patterns in our lives, like puppets on a string, because the unconscious need to do so is much stronger than the conscious need to change.

When we don't understand reality, why certain things happen to us, we may try to justify it with our beliefs, which stem from the same reality that originates the problem. The difference between reality and our beliefs defines the scope of our illness: the bigger the divergence between reality and our beliefs, the sicker we are. In order to heal we have to bring reality and our beliefs to match and overlap. At that point, apparently, disease is no longer needed and symptoms go into remission.

The event is not important: what is important is how we respond to it. To understand how an event has affected us we have to listen to how we give an account of it. Something can only resonate with whatever is already present (if there is nothing, there is no resonance). Therefore, an event capable of triggering a deeply felt response in me, a response that involves all levels of being, physical, emotional, mental and spiritual, is said to 'resonate' with my cellular structure, with the essence of who I am.

This resonance comes from the memories stored in my cells, what is already in me that comes from my ancestors and this is why the same event will resonate differently for different people, precisely because everyone has a different genetic background of ancestral memories.

This "DNA resonance" is therefore something I experience in response to some unusual circumstance and what is evoked in me, if I pay attention to it, goes beyond the scope of the event itself. My response to a DNA resonance triggering event may come from a memory I have inherited through many generations, from people of whom I know nothing. There will be a rather strong feeling state associated with a particular situation, and this is the DNA resonance itself. The next important thing to notice has to do with the set of circumstances that triggered this feeling, known as the triggering event.

DNA resonance responses happen in less than an eighth of a second, so, technically, they have no duration in time. It's the depth that matters. At conception, when the ovum has been fertilized, it contains all the information necessary for survival of that life. The new being must grow using its cellular endowment and its resources to protect itself. So the new organism uses some very basic strategy: when traumatic situations occur, on any level, the biological intelligence retrieves information on what to do by reading the information gathered the moment of conception, by that first cell. Somehow, psychobiology says, when out DNA cannot find instructions on how to cope with something in life, its intelligence seeks guidance based on what memories were stored in that first fertilized cell, based on parental and ancestral experience, and this creates the DNA resonance process I am attempting to describe.

In quantum physics we are told that communicating particles react to one another even when they are millions of miles apart. Our ancestors may be long gone, but their love for us is still reverberating through time and space, if we only listen. In the same way as a baby penguin can call and be found by its parents, among thousands of identical babies and parents, and in spite of the deafening clamor of seemingly identical calls, we can call to and resonate with, our ancestors' DNA, in order to find ways to navigate life's unpredictable twists and turns.

In other words, not all memories can be encoded and contained in what can be passed through cellular DNA. Life figured out a way to access a much larger data bank, when needed, by creating a process of resonance that can bypass physical limits of space and time.

This memory is then stored by using a certain kind of messenger molecule, called a neurotransmitter. The more intensely lived the experience is, emotionally, the more strongly it is impressed in the tissues. If a similar event subsequently evokes a similar response, the same thing happens: more of the same neurotransmitter is secreted onto the same tissue and the memory-based response becomes more deeply imprinted, reinforcing the structural belief system of the individual.

Since this now becomes part of the permanent "self", the physical self, the organism has made a rather substantial investment of time and resources in functioning from within this version of reality, the reality that requires this particular reactive configuration at the molecular and cellular level. This therefore becomes my "self", the self I perceive and am committed to, the self who believes things are as they are perceived.

So much is at stake at this point that changing my belief system becomes a cumbersome physiological task, no longer just a change of mind. It means developing new neuronal pathways, new dendrites, different connections, a different nervous system map. Most people prefer to hold on to the self they have invested in, which means the self that has developed as a result of cellular resonance.

To the point where, when committed to a certain believe system, we look for life situations that confirm our belief, even when this goes against our best interest.

We become invested in a certain reality because we have inherited an unfinished emotional sequence from our family, one that causes us to resonate with life events in a certain way. The good news is that, based on what kind of emotional experience we keep getting ourselves entangled in, we can figure out what conflict has not yet been resolved in our family. When we realize that an unresolved conflict might have been inherited, we finally understand why we cannot succeed if we keep trying to solve it as if it were ours.

THE PHYSIOLOGY OF SEPARATION

More than any other form of life, we are capable of adapting. To predators, to natural disasters, to inclement weather, to one another's cruelty. Genes are turned on or off as needed, to cope with whatever may come our way but one of the most difficult things a human being may have to cope with is being left behind by the tribe, left alone to fend for him or herself, left out of familiar places, activities and/or groups.

One of the most poignant biological dramas of evolution is symbolically reenacted every time we are displaced, abandoned, isolated, rejected, abused, orphaned, misunderstood, emotionally and/or physically separated from others.

And even though there may not be a lot of danger involved in living alone in the middle of a big city, for instance, one thing is certain: we didn't develop much of an ability to fend for ourselves through the millions of years that brought us forward all the way to modern times. Our ancestors readily and consistently chose group life rather than solitary life, probably because the daily necessities of survival were such that an individual alone was not likely to make it, while living in a group afforded him or her both the protection and resources he or she needed.

Urban life, with its artificial need for privacy and isolation, fosters a competitive outlook, tainted with mistrust of one's neighbors and even family members. And even though we may have accepted these unnatural parameters and think of our loneliness and alienation as a price worth paying in exchange for self-sufficiency, our bodies are certainly picking up the tab......and it seems very expensive.

We experience the trauma of this exile at the deepest level of being: body, mind, emotions, soul and spirit - we experience symptoms and suffer with diseases that affect our brains, our vital organs and functions, our emotional well being and our mental health. When we suffer, we cannot separate mind and body: we find a reflection of one in the other. Depending on where our focus is at any given time we may be more aware of one or the other, but the two are one continuum of experience where boundaries are arbitrary and flexible.

Paradise lost can be the loss of a mother, a father, a country, a child, a childhood, a career, a marriage, a religious belief, our own self-esteem, a job, a lover. It doesn't matter what is lost, when or why. It matters what happen to us as a result of that loss. It is well known that different people react differently to similar life's events, but in everyone's life there is a "refugee" experience, a reenactment of the myth of paradise lost.

THE REFUGEE SYNDROME

Through recent research in the work of Dr. Ryke Geerd Hamer, among others, I have come to understand what I call "The refugee syndrome". This is a complex cascade of physiological events that begins in the brain when our mind perceives the loss of something vital to us. This is not just losing one's favorite pair of earrings. I am talking about a loss that is perceived as a life threatening situation. When such a challenge occurs, the brain first, and then the body, respond with a remarkable precision and determination, bypassing intellect and reason, as well as concern for future repercussions.

The event is serious enough to mobilitate every survival resource available, including emergency programs the brain has never enacted before. Something has been stored in our DNA since life began, and that is the will to live. This will is strong enough to override normal genetic dictates. It is in fact capable of reprogramming DNA molecules as it sees fit, regardless of later consequences. When life is threatened in the moment, the moment is all that counts, and the brain sends a signal to the rest of the body that communicates just that.

For instance this can happen to a child who loses his or her mother to death, illness, emotional distance, etc. - or as a result of losing one's home because of war or displacement - or losing one's job and pension to company layoffs - or one's partner to infidelity or depression. The problem with us modern people is that we have lost a lot, perhaps more than we realize. Family, social structure, safety, spirituality, time with our children, time with our parents, time to follow our hearts, our country, our faith, etc. etc. The list is endless. In that sense, today's world is a world of refugees. Hence the ever increasing health care costs.

According to Dr. Hamer's research, in response to serious loss or separation, the brain also separates a group of neurons from the rest of itself. The refugee syndrome starts with an isolation of neurons. This protects the brain from more extensive damage, but also creates a splitting of consciousness. In the refugee syndrome, a group of neurons, now isolated from the rest of the brain, start acting as if they were on their own.

In response to the perceived survival threat - completely bypassing higher mental functions, like reason - the brain instructs the kidneys to implement water retention, to ensure immediate survival. Regardless of the fact that, in today's world, water is quite easy to find, even if we have been separated from our mother or if, like many other babies born to a modern family, we have been left in the care of a stranger.

The dramatic functional change resulting from such early stress may be temporary, depending on the severity and duration of the perceived separation and also depending on the caretaking skills of whomever we are left with. But it can become a permanent structural change, if the circumstances we are in continue to stress our system beyond its capacity to recover.

While this kind of adaptation response (i.e. water retention implemented to prevent lethal dehydration) could be helpful and life saving in an emergency (conserving water may be essential to our survival), it can become pathological when it is endured for too long, since it goes from temporary to irreversible.

This strategy on the part of the brain is automatic, archaic and unconscious - meaning that we cannot stop its implementation using our reasoning mind and its logical arguments. We understand it, but we are powerless to avoid it or reverse it once it is triggered. Along with it, I am convinced, many of the other so called "modern epidemics" ensue. Obesity, diabetes, heart disease, cancer...in my view, are all aspects of this effective life saving strategy gone too far.

This issue often becomes our neurosis, the core problem, the one dilemma or tragedy around which our life myth revolves - the loss of a mother or father, a job, a home, a mate, even a pet, can cause such severe physical reper-cussions that we may feel unable to cope, physically, emotionally and mentally. But what to say of collective losses, like that of the extended family system, replaced by the nuclear family. Or the loss of clean air and water and living trees? Or the constant threat of mass annihila-tion brought on by fear engendering political propaganda?

THE FAMILY'S SOUL

Each individual lives within his or her own animating space, a morphogenetic field, an etheric blueprint, and that space can be likened to a container of that individ-ual's life. Similar to the Russian Matrioskas, a series of identical but smaller dolls contained inside one another, we are like the smallest doll, at the center of gradually larger dolls, the largest one being our extended family.

We cannot unanimously agree with a definition of what a soul space is. In fact, some don't even believe that there is such a thing as a soul. I use this word because I don't have a better way of addressing the animating dynamic that is responsible for life's movement. But when I use the words "family's soul," I am actually referring to a feeling. Similar to what happens when we tune into a radio station, if we tune into our family, we get a sense of what it feels like to be part of that particular group of humans.

You can actually try that right now, at this moment, as you read these words....simply tune into that sense of loyalty, that visceral feeling of belonging to your tribe, that unique connection to one group of special people. And I believe you will shortly know what I am referring to.

When I was a child I used to believe that my family was the best in the world, my father the best father, my sister the best sister, etc., etc., in spite of the many disappointments I had to cope with, day in and day out, as a result of being part of that family. I remember wondering if I had a right to believe in our superiority, realizing how unfair it was to everyone else, but my feeling didn't go away until well into my teens.

A psychoanalytically oriented person might frame my self-appointed familial elitism more as a self-protective strategic adjustment than as an innate human tendency. And I might agree with that assessment, in my case, but I still believe that, even if we are angry with our family, even if we have broken all communications with them, we will find that sensation I am referring to, when we search for it deeply enough within our hearts.

Maybe, on the surface, it feels like a painful knot of resentments, all tangled up with frustration, or maybe like an impenetrable wall of cold steel. But regardless of what the surface emotional tone is, there is a place within us where only our family belongs. And that is true even for those people who were given up for adoption.

HOW TO EXPLORE ONE'S OWN FAMILY CONFIGURATION AND DNA RESONANCE PATTERNS

Take a sheet of paper and pretend it's a stage. Imagine the members of your nuclear family as the actors in a play. Then begin to draw circles on the paper, as if you were the play-writer, deciding were your actors should be standing. This is the opening scene and, depending on where you place everyone, your audience is going to get a sense of what this family is like, without anyone having to say a word.

Let this choice come from your heart. Don't think or ana-
lyze it too much. Just begin by placing your family members on stage, each one in the place that feels right to
you. Put initials under each circle, to represent each
member, like D for Dad, M for Mom, S for sister, B for
brother, and, if I were doing it for myself, RM for Roberta
Maria.

Place these circles on the paper as if they were all standing silently in a room. Imagine them to be the actors on a
stage, about to act your family's life as if it were a play
you have written, based on your inner image of it. To
make this part of the exercise complete, place an arrow
on each circle, only one for each person, to signify the direction the person is facing, looking at whom or what, in
relation to the room and everyone else in it.

After you are done positioning the circles, put down your
pen and look at what you drew. Then imagine standing
for a few minutes in each person's place and feel what it's
like to be that individual. You might find this exercise
quite revealing, I assure you.

You might find that everyone is looking in a different direction, for instance, and no one is looking at anyone

else. Or you might find that everyone is looking at Dad. Or you might find that Mom is turned around and looks away from the family. Or Grandma is standing too close to her son, your Father.

It is not possible for me to tell you what to do with this information, without being present while you try this exercise, but by looking at it yourself, you might realize something very important about yourself, maybe for the first time in your life, especially if you take the time to imagine what it would feel like to stand in everyone's place, as I said before.

The process is designed to shed light on the dark spots. Invariably, as a result of doing this exercise, people get in touch with revelatory information about themselves and their family, something they might have been aware of at a subconscious level but had not really looked at before they did the exercise, and yet, something vitally important in their life and indispensable for their well-being.

Human interactions are structured around an internal image. This image is formed and shaped, in part, by the life experiences to which the individual is exposed to during the first decade of his or her life. Based on this inner image the person makes life choices.

However, the internal image is also archetypal, in the sense that there is an ancient formula governing human relations, one that emerged out of biological and survival necessities. This archetypal structure is most likely reflected in the way the human body evolved.

This exercise works with the soul of the your family system and with many ancestors, beyond time. It identifies entanglements with other generations and allows resolutions to emerge for the individual, family, cultures, country and the world. Therefore, possibly, reprogramming the collective DNA, bringing forth from the past the wish for hope for peace contained within the heart of all who came before us.

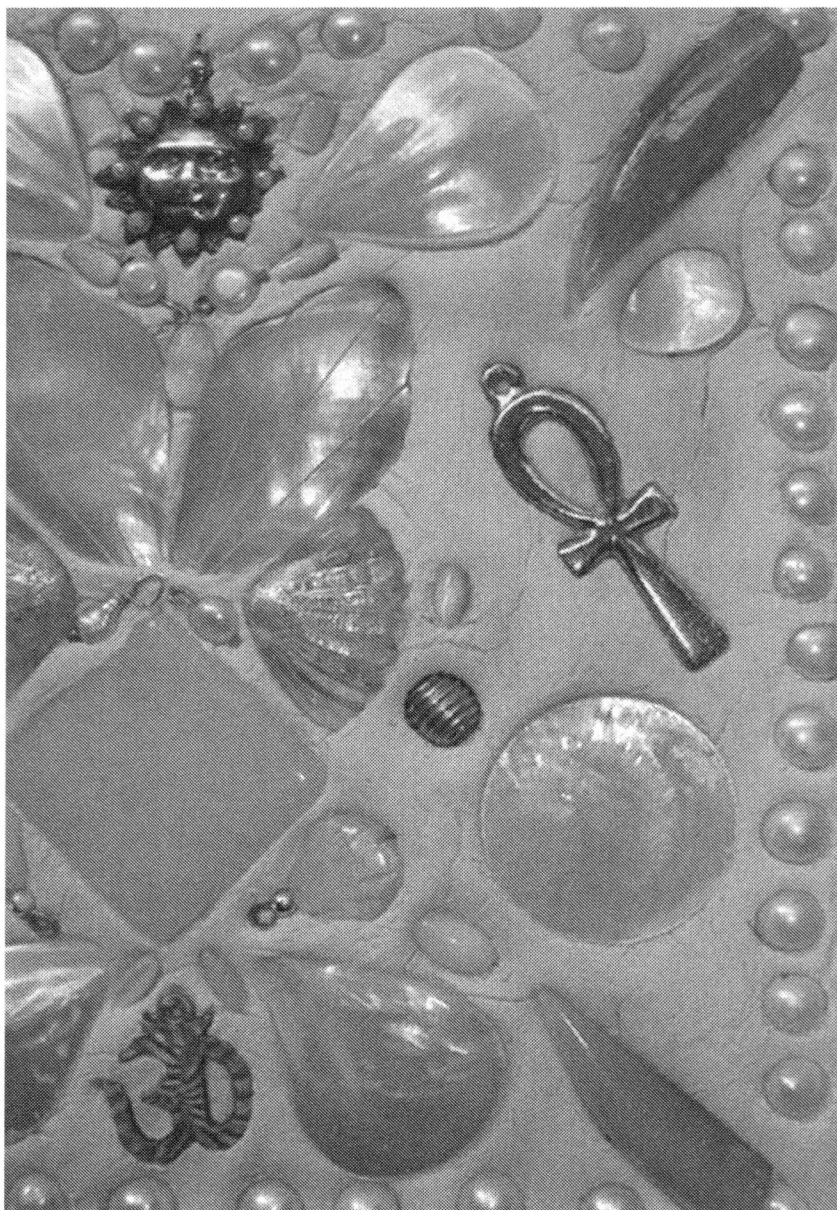

"Creation", by Roberta Maria Atti
Artist and Photographer

Chapter 6

Creativity Defined: Re-Creating the Human

Creativity could be called the "carte blanche" of the evolutionary game, the joker's wild card. "Do what you think is best, or do what your ancestors would have done, because there is nothing in the script that could help you with this problem", nature says when we are confronted with an unprecedented challenge. As humans we have a measure of genetic independence that allows for spontaneous response and so we can "invent" our way out of trouble, or into it, better than any other creature on the planet.

To create means bringing about something that did not exist before, through an act of will, motivated by desire or need, and fueled by intelligence. Animals create in order to facilitate survival. Nest building or tool making are examples of animals' creative gift. But humans are endowed with superb creative capabilities, as anyone can see by looking at how the planet has changed since humans made their appearance on it.

Unfortunately, an enormous amount of creative effort has been wasted or misused as a result of greed, ignorance and prejudice, but there is no time left, and no good enough reason, to blame ourselves for having almost destroyed the planet in creating things we do not need. Time is better spent, in my view, implementing a creativity that makes ecological and social sense. But before we get there, before we can bring about a sustainable way of life, we need to understand, and master, the creative process.

Thomas Berry, Ph.D., talks about reinventing the human and that may very well be our first step, if we are to save the planet. But what does it mean to reinvent ourselves? Is it just a clever description of an abstract wish, or is it possible to use our mind in ways we have not yet discovered? Can we literally reinvent our bodies? Our minds? Our souls?

Creativity is inherent in the universe. There cannot be a universe as we know it without it, in the same way as there could be no water without oxygen molecules. Imagine a static universe - one that is not born, does not die and never changes. Not easy, is it? We recoil from such an image, since the human mind perceives reality as the constant movement of evolution. Its opposite is frightening, in that, perhaps, it is one of the ways in which we imagine death.

The most astounding creative act is, of course, the universe itself. From an original spark, the most popular theory says, reverberations brought forth the creative impulse in ever more complex patterns of interactions, expanding into time and space for 15 billion years. Earth has existed for 4.5 billion years, or roughly one third of the entire universal creative venture.

Some anthropologists believe that humans have been around for as long as 10 million years. If that's true, 4 billion, 499,990 million years of creative expression on the planet has had nothing to do with us. Creativity on earth, for most of its existence, has been expressed by the elements that form the planet, minus human intelligence. Those are, according to physicist Brian Swimme, Ph.D., the lithosphere (rocks), the hydrosphere (water), and the atmosphere (air).

Organic life itself, the biosphere, according to most recent estimates, started approximately 3.5 billion years ago. Water, air and rocks, followed by plants and animals, brought forth earth's destiny with an exquisite creative flare, making the planet worthy of hosting the most evolved creature this elegant universe has been able to produce, at least as far as we know. The latest, and, by far, most powerful, sphere of creative force on earth is the "anthroposphere". In simple English: us.

What do I mean by a "sphere"? A sphere, in this context, means a set of dynamics that follow a specific pattern of interactive movement, internal and external. A sphere could be said to function based on some intelligent dictate inherent in the elemental matter governed by that sphere, whether it be liquid, solid or gaseous. A sphere also can be said to cause things to change permanently, perhaps to evolve, though interaction with itself and other spheres involved with different dynamics.

Can we say that spheres have consciousness? Maybe...and if water, for instance, has a consciousness, as Mr. Emoto suggests in his book "Messages from Water", what kind is it? Obviously, not human, but that should not deter us from speculating. Can we say that

perhaps earth showed a desire to exist and to evolve, before humans did? And can we say this desire seems to be
present in the atoms and molecules that come together,
and stay together, to form structures suitable to earthly
life?

Everything that happened, from the birth of this planet
until now, is so unlikely to happen by coincidence that I
feel safe imagining a creative impulse inherent in its matter, separate and different from, human creativity. In
other words, life, in my view, wanted to happen on earth
regardless of the human sphere of existence. Humans,
from that perspective, are but a joint venture, a kind of
experiment on the part of life and of the planet.

After billions of years of relatively stable creative momentum, whereby life on earth had become self-sustaining
and self-perpetuating, it seems that the intelligence governing the evolutionary process decided to take a great
leap of faith.

It must have gone something like this: what if - Earth
said - now that I have learned how to keep myself alive, I
give one creature more creative power than anything or
anyone has ever had before? And what if I allow this crea-

ture to rule my future, and the future of all other creatures, animal, plant or mineral? Could that creature possibly bring me to a better place than the one I am headed for?

If I am right about the intelligence that opted for taking that risk, what we have now is an experiment gone awry, at least in some ways. This perspective, by the way, has been hypothesized by Brian Swimme, Ph.D., a renowned physicist, among many others before me.

I don't mean to sound pessimistic or hopeless. My wish is to create hope, in fact. I do mean to point out that we are the most creative dynamic ever brought forth on earth and, as far as we know, in the universe. Our need to create is relentless. It drives us to the point of obsession. We create constantly and we create compulsively. In a way, we are condemned to create.

And there is nothing wrong with that. In fact, it is the greatest gift I could possibly ask for, to be able to create the reality I wish for. A reality filled with good things, like health and joy and freedom and peace, for myself and for those I love.

And I am not alone in believing that, on some level, every human being wants to create that same reality, even if the ways we go about it may seem incongruent with the desired goal. I may be naive, but I believe every human, ultimately, wants to create Heaven on earth.

But then....why do we bring about the opposite? Why do we live in fear and despair, when all we want is happiness? What goes wrong in the creative process that, in spite of our being so powerfully creative, we manifest the exact opposite of what we set out to do?

I am convinced that the answer to these difficult questions is not as complicated as we may at first believe. I am convinced: the problem, at least in part, stems from the fact that we do not yet know how it is that we create. It is as if we were given a race car to drive and we tried to ride it like a bicycle. All we have to do is figure out the commands. If we do that, and it may not be nearly as difficult as we think, we may just find a way to lead ourselves out of danger.

HOW DO WE CREATE

Creating can be compared to dreaming, in the sense that all the factors necessary to complete the process are held within the mind at all times. Past, present and future are non-sequential aspects of a dream, rather than containers for its expression, and so it is with creativity. To put it more simply, we must not worry about lacking what we need in order to create what we want. Everything we could possibly need is always available. What is required of us is a sufficient degree of creative intention, along with patience and persistence. But the raw material is never lacking, since it is always present in the form of energy, in the same way as all images needed to dream are available in our mind before we start dreaming.

A dream is all there at once, even though, from the dreaming mind's perspective, different parts of it appear to follow one another in a sequence. So a dream happens only within the inner mental landscape, the imagination, and is created by concepts contained therein, like every other function and/or structure of that mind. Creating happens in the same way as dreaming, except for one aspect: the mental landscape is no longer limited to the imagination. It also involves intention, choice and bodily perception.

Whatever the mind assembles through the creative impulse, reverberates into the physical sea of energy and creates a wave. This wave magnetizes molecules and various particles of matter, until a reflection of the creative thought has been assembled also on the physical plane, to match the original mental image.

Quite often, along the way, since creating happens in a sequence, the mental blueprint evolves and changes from the prototype, and this is normal. The finished product then results in a percolated essence of the original idea. The point I am making is that, in order for us to have a bicycle, the bicycle had to be created in someone's mind first. And what we are now exploring is just how do we cause things to precipitate from mental dreamland to day to day reality, until the bicycle we imagined is right there in front of us, sparkling with our creative momentum.

Perhaps we should start by acknowledging that, even in so called objective reality, while it is impossible to describe cause and effect without giving the impression that the former precedes the latter, their separation in time is a deception of the senses. This is one of the hardest concepts to grasp, for most people. And yet, it is one of the most important.

In reality cause and effect are simultaneous events. In other words, it appears that life happens through a sequence of consecutive events, while in reality it is happening in one event that doesn't exist anywhere within time, but rather creates the illusion of time within itself, as it emerges out of nothing.

Creativity causes the precipitation of a thought into a form perceivable by the senses. But the ideation that precedes creation is both the originator and container of the time and space into which its precipitated reflection becomes solid. This way of understanding reality may not be immediately accessible to our mental learning tool. It is nonetheless congruent with the latest discoveries in physics.

The universe, and everything born therein, beginning to end, is much more similar to a dream than to the reality we imagine it to be, appearing to be real in this way only to the mind that is perceiving it. Knowing this is important, and we shall soon see why.

To better grasp this idea let us imagine that we are hearing the word "water" in our mind. We can evoke the sound of this word using our auditory memory to activate the vibration caused by repeating this word silently in our mind. Then let us conjure up visual images of water: the taste of sea water versus the taste of fresh water; the smell of the earth after a thunderstorm; the feel of a warm bath after a long day.

Pretty soon we realize how the silent sounding of the word "water" sets in motion a whole host of inner experiences and imaginal landscapes. The only difference between imagination and a dream is that the former is structured by choice, while the latter, for most people, is not.

Please keep in mind that everything we evoke by silently sounding the word "water" is present in our imagination already - at the same time as the word itself and also what we imagine in relation to it. Each new image seems to be brought forth in a sequential pattern, but it is only our awareness of that image that happens in a sequence. All images are already there to begin with, while our way of noting them gives us the impression that they follow one another like pearls on a necklace. We can only perceive one pearl at a time, but the necklace is there all at once.

At the moment we choose to evoke images connected to a word we focus our awareness on something which is there all the time, even when we are not aware of it. In that sense our awareness functions similarly to a flashlight. In a dark room full of objects, the objects are there regardless of whether we can see them or not. Once we shine a flashlight on them we can see them and they appear in a consecutive sequence, depending on what we choose to shine the light on and when. But the objects are not coming into existence in that sequence. They already exist, all at the same time, from before we started to shine the light on them.

But if this is the way things are, where are the objects, people, situations, events and other things we perceive and react to? Do we create them? Or do they exist of their own independent life, outside of our control? And where is our awareness of them? In our minds? With them? Or by itself?

We could say that all there is is an infinite sea of energy, vibrating at different frequencies. In that sea, energy perceives itself by creating the illusion of existing in many different forms. This differentiation makes it possible for perception to occur. If everything were homogenous to perception, there would be no awareness of being, because awareness would be all there is. So, within the illusion of separateness, it seems as though things exist on the outside and people have individual consciousness that can never be bridged to and merged into. We seem to be able to touch one another, sometimes deeper than other times, but never could we truly become one.

And yet, when we look at the way things are on the physical level, we are presented with a very different picture. What if things were like this: there is one mind and that mind is everywhere at every moment. Depending on where, from within the mind, awareness is, it will have a different perspective of the rest of itself, thereby creating the separation between one and the other parts of itself, as in observer and observed.

Therefore everything is an aspect of the mind that perceives it, rather than a location, an object or a life form outside of it. Everything is an aspect of the creative mind that dreams the original creative event, which is the universe. A person other than myself is but a part of me, seen from a particular perspective I call myself.

All of this taken into account, how can we define creativity? Do we create reality? Or does reality create us? The answer is that there is an endless creative loop, whereby we create reality which creates us so that we can create it. Nothing exists that has not existed as a thought first. Nothing exists on the solid level without an energy matrix behind it to hold it together in that form.

And the matrix is composed of intention, or desire, imagination, will, intelligence and love. All of those ingredients, and certainly more, seem to be necessary to create a force field strong enough to attract, coordinate, organize and sustain form. It is my belief that without any one of them, creation cannot happen. Even when we are talking about purely physical phenomena, such as creation of a star or a galaxy.

We tend to limit our definition of love, will and intelligence to the human expression of these powerful forces. But if we could relinquish, just for a moment, our self-appointed supremacy and allow for a wider meaning of the word, we can easily extend our mind until we perceive a kind of love expressing itself through the way trees grow and the way stars collide and the way atoms hold on to one another without apparent reason.

If we can get to a level of open mindedness whereby an event brought forth by gravity can still be called creative (i.e. a waterfall), we may be on our way to learning how to create what we truly wish for, instead of succumbing to powerlessness and frustration.

An Italian proverb says "no leaf moves without God's permission". If everything is an aspect of the mind that perceives it, and in which it exists, and if that mind is dreaming (creating a dream), how do we introduce the element of conscious choice into the dream, so that we can control what happens in it? How do we call images forth in the dream? Do we think them? Do we see them? Do we say them? Or all of the above?

Is it possible to create the reality I want by focusing my awareness on it, rather than becoming aware of whatever happens and calling that reality?

Our ancestors could not connect the birth of a child to conception. To them, since they had no way of connecting cause and effect, the two events seemed unrelated and a human birth was attributed to mysterious forces, perhaps divine, perhaps natural. Today, our eyes are able to access the image of a developing fetus, all of the way back to the first union of the gametes. To us pregnancy and birth of a child are the predictable result of successful conception, chemically and biologically consistent with what we have learned about the human body.

Perhaps, by the same token, what we consider mysterious is but another veil of a reality we are yet to discover. Or have we reached the limits of what is empirically knowable? How far into the atom can we go, before we find God? Or will God continue to elude us, one veil of illusion after another, until all that's left will be a mirror? Or maybe nothing?

The problem is....we don't know how powerful we are, yet. We don't see that we are co-creators with the Creator. We are so afraid of our magnificence that we would rather destroy ourselves than take our seat at Mount Olympus, side by side with Divinity.

We want peace and we create war. We want health and we create disease. We want justice and we create exploitation. We are like an adolescent monkey that has discovered the secret of how to make fire and is having a great deal of fun burning everything up, including its own home. Fire is what we use to create and destroy. Fire is the tool and the very essence of our creativity.

What do I mean by that? We have discovered how, by using fire in a certain way, we can extract the energy contained in matter. This gives us power over the earth. We are burning up every bit of life we can find, because we are so fascinated with what we can do with the energy we are able to extract from it, without looking at the consequences of our enthusiastic, if inconsiderate, use of creativity.

To explain in a concrete example how creativity works in humans I will now share with you how I discovered my own creative power. I hope this will help you discover your own.

I once saw a beautiful dog. The most beautiful dog I had ever seen. I had never had a dog of my own and this, I decided, was the one I had been waiting for. However, this magnificent animal being a Great Pyrenees, I soon realized that buying a dog of this breed was out of my financial reach at the time. So I started to create the picture of my dog in my mind. I imagined him everyday, in every detail. How old he would be. His personality. The look in his eyes. Everything.

It took six months, but one day I got a call from a friend who told me there was a dog, named Sydney, who sounded perfect for what I was looking for, and he was being given up for adoption, for free.

I drove six hours, picturing in my mind my first encounter with this creature I had dreamed into existence. And, when I saw him, I recognized him immediately: finally, here was my dog, coming towards me, exactly as I had imagined him im my mind. Sydney lived with me for 15 years, a very long life for a dog of this breed, and to this day he represents one of the most successful acts of creativity in my life, the most important lesson on creativity I ever learned and one of the greatest companion creatures of my earth journey. Did Sydney also create me in his mind? I wonder...I believe he did, but I cannot tell you for sure. I believe we created each other, with so much love and joy, that our life together could truly be called a gift from Heaven. This is Creativity with a Capital C.

In the same way as we would need a different type of vehicle to travel by water than what we need to travel on land, when we first learn how to create consciously, we might want to try leaving our wheels behind and opt for taking up the ors. This is precisely where we find ourselves today. In the sense that creativity requires a mental shift.

Our intellect has served us so well. It has taken us to the edge of knowledge, give or take a few more discoveries. We have mastered observation and deduction. We have conquered the smallest unit of matter and gone beyond, where matter, time and space no longer exist. And we are still struggling with figuring out what to eat that won't make us fat or unhealthy.

Perhaps the inevitable paradox of a species gifted with divinity and trapped in mortality, we conquer the moon before we master the use of our own brain. We can see to

the farthest reaches of the universe, but we can't see ourselves as we would like to be.

I suggest we may want to try imagining ourselves as we
wish to be, just to see what happens.

And I am not talking about positive affirmations and positive thinking. In my opinion those solutions offer but
temporary and partial relief from an underlying discom-
fort that cannot be assuaged through discipline and
methodologies. I believe we need to master creativity in its
fullest potential and expression.

Some hesitation and doubt are understandable. Creativity, at this level, is a new mental landscape, one we have
not explored before, except for mystics and visionaries.
But the shadow of our intellectual success, in the form of
our technological wasteland, is quickly catching up with
us, determined to confront us with what we have sacrificed in order to subdue and conquer the natural world
and turn it into a dry, sterile human friendly artificial
version of what was once alive and bountiful.

This is not to be seen as a mistake worthy of punishment, in my view, but rather as a necessary step in growing up as a species, from clumsy adolescent primates to responsible stewards of the planet.

Can we imagine salvation out of this? Can we imagine ourselves healthy? Not alone and endowed with self-defeating supremacy, victoriously superior while everything else is dying, but alive and filled with an abundance of life, together with everything else. Can we envision what we want the most? Peace, love, faith, trust, brotherhood and sisterhood, protection of non human forms of life, a future for our children's children.

I say, if we can imagine it, it can be done. History says so. Everything that exists today had to be imagined by someone before it could be realized. A sweater, a building, a garden, a rifle, an atomic bomb.

The same principle applies in positive as it does in negative. I believe we can do a lot more with our minds than we ever thought possible, once we learn a few simple things about creativity, how to develop it and how to use it.

The first step is imagining the world we would like to create, exactly as we would like it to be. What would your ideal reality look like? Dare to imagine it, as John Lennon proposed so gracefully in his lyrics, and you might just find it in front of you one of these days, as you pull up your shades in the morning and look at the world from your bedroom window.

Wouldn't that be just like a dream?

www.ingramcontent.com/pod-product-compliance
Lightning Source LLC
Chambersburg PA
CBHW051846040426
42447CB00006B/719